To Ava,

*Foreword by Les & Ona Brown "The 1st Family of Motivation"*

# BE AMAZING!

## A GUIDE TO BECOMING THE BEST VERSION OF YOURSELF

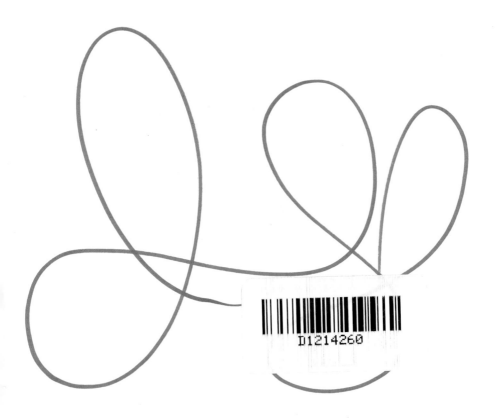

This page intentionally

left blank

by

*Foreword by Les & Ona Brown "The 1st Family of Motivation"*

# BE AMAZING

A GUIDE TO BECOMING THE BEST VERSION OF YOURSELF

Author & Illustrator:

## John R.F. Humphreys

Editor:

## Dave Clark

Foreword:

## Les & Ona Brown

## *"The 1st Family Of Motivation"*

Amazing John John
2017

*Foreword by Les & Ona Brown "The 1st Family of Motivation"*

# BE AMAZING

A GUIDE TO BECOMING THE BEST VERSION OF YOURSELF

Author and Illustrator: John R.F. Humphreys

All Rights Reserved.

Copyright © 2017 by  (John R.F. Humphreys)

Humphreys, John R.F., 2017

**BE AMAZING** : A Guide To Becoming The Best Version Of Yourself;

John R.F. Humphreys

1. Self Help – Motivational
2. Entrepreneurship – self-help;
3. Children – encouragement
4. Humphreys, John R.F. II Title
5. Amazing John John

Special discounts are available on quantity purchases by corporations, associations, educators, and others. For details, contact the publisher at Beyond Publishing BeyondPublishing.net.

Manufactured and printed in the United States of America distributed globally by BeyondPublishing.net

**BEYOND**
PUBLISHING

For information or to order more copies for you or your team go to: BeyondPublishing.net

New York | Los Angeles | London | Sydney

Library of Congress Control Number: 2017961756

First Printing: 2017

ISBN: 978-1-947256-09-5 Perfect Bound

Printed in the United States of America

First Edition

# ENDORSEMENTS

"Scientists need to find a way to clone John John & his ideas for how to Be Amazing. As someone who has spent his career inspiring students, educators & even business owners on ways to be amazing, I'm excited about the impact & influence this book will have on a generation filled with unlimited potential & boundless opportunities. A word of warning... Don't be fooled by the youthfulness of the author. This is a book for anyone who wants to stretch their limits and discover new insights that will change their lives forever."

*Steve Spangler*
*Science Influencer*
*Hall of Fame Speaker*
*Emmy-Award Winning TV Host*

"It takes a lot of focus, discipline, and hard work to thrive in the NFL for 6 years. This book is filled with ancient wisdom and practical solutions, some of which I used to succeed in professional sports. You'd be wise to learn the lessons in BE AMAZING!"

*Frank D. Murphy,*
*Wide Receiver (6 years NFL) Tampa Bay Buccaneers,*
*Houston Texans, Miami Dolphins*
*Author & National Motivational Speaker*

"Think of him as Bill Nye, only cuter and shorter."

*Nathan Bonilla-Warford*
*OD Bright Eyes Family Vision Care*

"They say publishing your book makes you "The Expert" Amazing John John shows he is one by writing BE AMAZING! 5 Stars John John! A rare treat to get such wisdom from an 8 year old boy.

This is one of those books you want to have on your nightstand, in your car, taped to the bathroom mirror. It's your morning shot of caffeine to keep you ahead of your day! BE AMAZING lives up to it's name!"

*Gerry Robert, Bestselling Author*
*Publish A Book And Grow Rich*

"The very first time I met John John, I realized, he was an inspiration to all that would have the pleasure of being in his presence. In a simple description, John John has an amazing way of encouraging you to focus on your end goal. His youthfulness creates a fun yet challenging manifestation to conquer your fears. His knowledge and beliefs of success is on a level that dares you to get out of your comfort zone and create a better version of yourself. As the editor of IBA Success Magazine, I strongly believe that feeding your mind valuable content not only enriches your life but empowers your future. After reading Be Amazing, I immediately felt a surge of energy to reevaluate and execute my goals. There is nothing in life more rewarding then the power of self-realization, when you can realize you have the potential to create the life you want, your dreams become reality. And your reality creates a life you can be proud of. This book will do all the above for you, it's a must read for all ages and I look forward to continue sharing with all I come in contact with. Do yourself a favor and take charge of your life by reading Be Amazing. Thank you John John!"

*Jennifer Yon*
*Founder & Editorial Director IBA Success Magazine*

"If you are looking for a way to be inspired to do your very best, then this book is a great place to start. Be Amazing is a simple yet powerful tool to train the brain and attitude to turbo-charge your success journey…By using his method, John John has been able to develop a budding career as a motivational speaker, actor, educator, and magician."

*Les & Ona Brown "The 1st Family Of Motivation"*

"BE AMAZING" is definitely a Guide To Becoming The Best Version Of Yourself. The very young author, the Amazing John John, has found a way to help others. His guide offers a unique journey and inspires the reader to live your dreams. Nine chapters uses pictures and quotes, and his words. The book provides a path for you to become inspired."

*Robert Neff,*
*Writer/Photographer/Artist, PelicanBeakon.com*

"John John is an amazing 9 year old author that is unforgettable. He is a true inspiration to anyone wanting to persevere and succeed in the speaking world. His book will lift your spirits. You're in for a real treat!"

*Omar Periu, Best-Selling Author & Speaker*

"Old folks always told me, "if you only knew what I know?" John John already knows what some never find out at His young age. If you stay positive you can reach your goals while having fun. You'll "BE AMAZING". This young man has the recipe for a fruitful life."

*Les McDowell*
*Creator of Dry Creek Voted Best Family Friendly Series*
*Cable Faxes Awards in NYC & Winner of a CMA Award*
*2003 Number 1 show major market*

"John John really hit the home run with this book. It's a very inspirational and positive book that will help in many areas of life. From professional athletes to kids and parents you will get some wonderful takeaways that will last you a lifetime. Highly recommend this for everyone looking to better themselves."

*Jason Romano, Former MLB Player*

"This kid is the next JT Foxx - Get his book to BE AMAZING!"

*JT Foxx, The World's #1 Wealth Coach*

"What an example for kids around the world you are John John! This is a powerhouse read and something every parent should grab for the kids and read it to them. Thanks super star for sharing your gifts with all of us! Look forward to watching you rise and all that are impacted by you!"

*Danelle Delgado*
*CEO Life Intended, World-Renowned Speaker,*
*Ambitious Mother of 3*

I LOVE this book and I am an Official RAVING FAN of the Amazing John John! I'm called to raise up Million Dollar Gurus around the world. I search for that unique combination of Message, Mission, Maturity and Communication Mastery and, as you will experience in this book, John John has it all! I encourage you to Devour this Book!

*James MacNeil, The Guru Builder*

"John John is taking risks at such a young age and learning not to give up at accomplishing his dreams."

*Jeffrey Alan*
*The Man of Mystery (performance Artist)*

I highly recommend reading this book. This will not only motivate but encourage the younger generation to set high standards for themselves, practice personal development, and be more involved in the community and make an impact at any age. John John is a trend setter for the youth and is using magic, motivation and learning the new and cool thing to do for all ages. Better Body Better Life approved.

*"Coach Cody"*

"This book was fun to read. I have worked with John John on my movie Nekoda and this kid is "AMAZING". He follows direction well, is a great actor and is a fine young man who will grow up to do "AMAZING" things in his life and he has already started! Read this book and follow this young man's career, he is a speaker, a magician. an actor an so much more. This book is very inspirational to young and old, I am 56 years young and I enjoyed this book from start to finish.

*Joel D. Wynkoop, King of the B Movies*

"Wow. This book it beyond what could be imagined by the regular person. An 8 year old inspiring others to be their best! It goes to show you that the brain of a child knows no limits. This book is a great reminder of how important it is to live life without blocks, but to always keep our inner child ALIVE."

*Lili Serrano*
*Principal Digital Marketer iMarketing Made Simple*

"God made the Small to Lift us Big! Amazing John John charms with his wit, wisdom and warmth. Step Up with John John and Be Amazing!"

*Shradha, Author of Witness the Breakthrough*

This book is an absolute must read for kids and parents who want to live their best lives! John John is not only an incredibly confident and inspiring young man, he has also discovered the keys to breaking through fear and accomplishing huge goals...and with his guidance you can too!

*Chelsea Matthews*
*Co-Author of "Let's Fight About Money"*
*Licensed Financial Professional*

Age is irrelevant when it comes to John John. He possesses the wisdom, passion and drive some people don't acquire in a lifetime. His enthusiasm, inspiration and excitement for life is boundless and infectious. You will feel amazing any time you're with John John and you will be amazing after reading his book.

*Mary Rachel Dudley, Actor/Producer*

I knew JohnJohn was going to be a shredder the minute I shook the young man's hand. His enthusiasm and drive was unlike that of any other person's that I had ever met.

Surfing can be an intimidating sport due to its unpredictable nature, and JohnJohn not only adapted, but thrived in the hostile environment. We had a lot of time to chat in between sets, and I was blown away by his intellect of the universe and drive to become an astronaut. We all know that his career choice is a popular one among kids, but there was this twinkle in his eye that confirmed that this grom is destined to be great.

*Tyler Kelsey*
*Personal Trainer/Surf Instructor*

Pretty Amazing piece of work, and now I want to hear and see your presentation! I firmly believe you are a blessing to this crazy place we call Earth. Congratulations on your first book, and I look forward to reading many more by you in the future. It will be entertaining to watch your journey!

*Nadya DePontbriand, Editor*

A great little book that not only gets you back in touch with your younger self but reminds your older self to step up the game and push fear aside.

*Charles Deguara*
*CEO @ IPOP Network*

John John's incredible insight to life and the future is valuable to both young and old.

*Charlie Cina*
*Private Labeled Virtual Training Systems*
*LightSpeedVT.com*

"Every parent and child must read BE AMAZING to see how they can make a huge impact in the world!"

*Bardi Toto, New York Times*
*Best-Selling Author "The Power of Asking"*

"BE AMAZING is full of timeless truths that will change your life. John John will inspire you to discover and become the very best you. Let go of your fear and make the impossible, possible. It's like magic!"

*Gary Barker*
*Founder of The Magic Emporium*

BE AMAZING! This book captures the optimism of the human who listens to their heart, and does not choose to "follow the herd". This book is packed with wit, wisdom, humor, healing-energy, perspective and passion.

What I love best about "BE AMAZING" is it affirms that we all have our own values, our own dreams, our own way of 'showing up' authentic. John-John tells us that "Every brain is wired differently. ... What you do in life and what you learn, literally rewires your brain. Remember the things that make us different are the things that make us strong."

Reading this book encourages all of us to examine and conquer your fears, learn secrets to success, and reach your goals, while having fun, living our dreams and rekindling the innate human passion for learning, exploring, and "adding to" life itself.

*Rob Tamboia*
*President of Champion Mindset Events*
*A division of Strategic Seminars & Training, Inc.*

It's not often that you get to hear from an amazing and incredible young author, speaker and talent like Amazing John John. BE AMAZING, takes you on a journey to help you believe, escape your fear and make your plans for success. This book helps you to act on your plans, continue life long learning and most of all, help others while having a good time doing it. BE AMAZING will help you become a better version of yourself and you too, can "BE AMAZING".

*Dr. Robert Lemon*
*Professional Speaker, Best Selling Author*
*"Now Is Your Time"*

John John is a lifetime ahead of his peers and light years ahead of most adults. A must read for all!

*Lee Owens*
*Commercial and Residential*
*Real Estate Entrepreneur*

In this day and age of lost dreams, low self-esteem, and self entitlement there is now an answer to lead you back to a better life! John John is an inspiration for all ages. The book is not only amazingly written, but it is a self check into reality. It's time for all to step away from your social media - READ this book and become the best person you can. It's a guideline to change your life and an opportunity to improve the lives of all others around you! This should be mandatory reading for every school!

*Captain Shawn Tucy*

Thank you so much to my family for helping me achieve my goals and live my dreams. Without your love, guidance, support, and patience, I would not be able to do all the wonderful things I do. I love you.

# CONTENTS

Acknowledgements 19

Foreword 21

About The Author 23

Preface 25

Chapter 1: Believe 27

Chapter 2: Escape Your Fear 33

Chapter 3: Access Your Imagination 43

Chapter 4: Make Your Plan 49

Chapter 5: Act On Your Plan 53

Chapter 6: Zest For Life Is Learning 61

Chapter 7: Inner Child 71

Chapter 8: Need To Help Others 79

Chapter 9: Good Times 85

BE AMAZING Song 91

BE AMAZING Workbook 93

BE AMAZING – TTD Worksheets 103

BE AMAZING – Goals Worksheets 109

Index 113

Notes 115

Glossary 121

# ACKNOWLEDGEMENTS

I would like to thank all who have helped, guided, and taught me. I am forever grateful for all I have learned and all who have taken their time to teach me something new, explained something, or have shown me something cool. With that said, I can never thank everyone by name, but there are many of you who have helped to make this book possible.

This book would have never happened if it were not for my family and all of their support, encouragement, and patience. Thank you for everything you did to make this possible.

Thank you to The 1st Family Of Motivation for writing the foreword for this book. Mr. Les Brown for his coaching and motivational quotes, and Miss Ona Brown, The Message Midwife, for her coaching, guidance, suggestions, and expertise.

Thank you to The Les Brown Institute and Les Brown Maximum Achievement Team Members for all your encouragement and guidance.

Thank you to Mr. Dave Clark for editing my book and helping with the music writing for my Be Amazing song. You are the best piano teacher ever. Well, actually the best teacher, ever.

Thank you to Peter Zayas for your graphic artist skills and for helping me to make my Amazing John John logo dream a reality.

Thank you to John Lennon and Shel Silverstein whose works inspired me in creating the illustrations for this book.

Thank you to all the people whose quotes I have used in this book for making such memorable statements. May they continue to encourage and inspire others. I can only hope to one-day come close to doing the same.

Thank you to the authors of the poems and songs that I reference throughout the book. May your examples inspire the readers to learn more.

Thank you to the great people who have done such awesome and selfless things that shaped our history and left their bread crumbs to success in helping us all to succeed.

Thank you all for the fun jokes that have been circulating around bringing laughter into the world, may they give you a chuckle.

# FOREWORD

If you are looking for a way to be inspired to do your very best, then this book is a great place to start. Be Amazing is a simple yet powerful tool to train the brain and attitude to turbocharge your success journey.

Self-development is something we must dedicate ourselves to on a daily basis, which is why you and your family should keep this book close. This information will guide you and keep you on track toward your next level of greatness.

Be Amazing, with its companion workbook, is a study for people young and old to be inspired to take action and become the best version of themselves. Even more seasoned participants will have a rejuvenation of the role of positive attitude and action force in daily life.

John John's unique perspective gives insight well beyond his years, as he is truly an old soul. By using his method, John John has been able to develop a budding career as a motivational speaker, educator, and magician.

Les & Ona Brown
"The 1st Family Of Motivation"

# ABOUT THE AUTHOR

John R.F. Humphreys (John John) is a motivator, educator, actor, model, science kid, magician, pianist, singer, and all around happy Earthling.

John John is making his mark as the youngest motivational speaker. He loves to learn new things and share that information with others.

Now 8 years old, John John has partnered with Mr. Les Brown an international motivational speaker who has been named one of the top five speakers in the world. John Humphreys is a founding member of the Les Brown Maximum Achievement Team. He helps to encourage positive transformation, by inspiring and motivating audiences.

John John recently has been involved with his speaking and acting career. He has been performing on stage with many amazing people like Mr. Les Brown, Miss Ona Brown, Mr. Omar Periu, NFL players like Frank Murphy, Seneca McMillan, Ron Dixon, Michael Coe, and Lee Paige. Some of his recent video and movie credits include Reba McEntire's music video Pray for Peace, and the movies Turtle Tale, Elixir Madragora, Swift Justice, Sweet Tooth, and Nekoda.

It is said that you have to get out of your comfort box to be able to change, grow, and reach new heights. John John says "You have to get so far out of your box that you do not even know where the box is."

John John wants to help to transform people's lives for the better, help people conquer their fears, and reach their goals. He has written his first book called BE AMAZING! A Guide to Becoming the Best Version of Yourself.

He loves to have fun and feels it is important to work together, help people, and keep our beaches clean. It only takes one person's actions to start something, but with lots of good people, working toward a common goal, anything can be accomplished!

It is hard for everyone to get together and have a play date packed with fun activities. So, John John asks, "What if I do the activities and video it. Then people can see how much fun learning can be?" Hopefully people will be encouraged to try new things, learn something new, and have fun doing it! There are fun clips, educational information, and entertaining videos! So please subscribe to JohnJohnsVideos on YouTube to stay up to date with new videos. You can also like the Amazing John John Fan Page on Facebook and follow him on Twitter and Instagram @AmazingJohnJohn

# PREFACE

Hello and thank you for purchasing my book. I love to learn new things and share them with others. I have written this book because I want you to Be Amazing. I truly want you to become the best version of yourself. Why, you ask? I have not even met you, you say. While this may be true, I feel we are all connected as human beings. With this said, if we all work together and achieve our goals, then we can all have a healthy, happy life. What a wonderful world that will be. I have written this book because I know I will probably never meet everyone, but my book can be read by everyone.

Be Amazing is a unique journey full of positivity, encouragement, and guidance. It takes you from the first step of the journey…Begin, all the way to achieving your goals, celebrating accomplishments, and enjoying the… Good Times of Life! This book encourages gratitude, kindness, and success. Through personal examples, stories of great people, jokes, poetry, inspirational quotes, and songs, it inspires the reader to overcome everyday challenges and fears. Each of us from birth develops special unique gifts and talents. When you finish reading this book, you will be on the path to success and to becoming the best version of yourself. Reading this book directs you to examine and conquer your fears, learn secrets to success, and reach your goals, while having fun. This book is for you, the reader, to be inspired to live your dreams by igniting the passion for learning and encouraging you to learn more.

May you enjoy reading this book as much as I have enjoyed writing it!

# Chapter 1

# BELIEVE

## BEGIN BY BELIEVING
## AND BUILD ON IT...

"*A journey of a thousand miles begins with the first step.*"

–LAO TZU–

Congratulations, you have taken the first step...Thank you for choosing to be the best most amazing version of yourself! Just by starting to read this book, you are on your way. Once you decide to do something, amazing things happen and your mind subconsciously starts working to make it a reality. As you take steps toward that goal, you start getting the universe on your side. That is powerful! It is important to understand this.

Every brain is wired differently. This is part of what makes you unique. Celebrate it! What you do in life and what you learn literally rewires your brain. Remember the things that make you different make you strong. Everyone is unique and thinks differently, but we all have similar wants and needs.

*"If you fell down yesterday, stand up today."*

H.G. WELLS

It is a good idea to do something emotionally relevant to reset your attention. That is why one hears about the 10 minute rule, which states you should check yourself every 10 minutes. Are you smiling? Are you having fun? Are you working toward your goals? If yes, continue. If no, regroup and make a change. Take a minute to reevaluate what you are doing and adjust your attitude. This can simply mean smile or get up and shake out the negative. You can also go for a walk, tell a joke and laugh, or just simply review your goals.

How many tickles does it take to make an octopus laugh?

Ten tickles.

Every day brings you new choices and opportunities. In order to take full advantage of all the wonderment that lies ahead, you must first be in the right mindset to succeed. When you wake up early in the morning, this is your special moment to grab hold of the day. Love your inner child. Let each morning be like Christmas. Open your eyes with happiness and run out to meet the day. Check your stockings first. This means look over your to do list and check off the first thing: wake up. Check! Next, get up and make your bed. Check! If you make your bed as soon as you get up, you have started the day with something already accomplished. Go check it off your list of things to do. This not only gives you a sense of accomplishment, it starts the day off on a good foot. Next: brush your hair and teeth. Now the day has just begun, but you have already accomplished the top few things on your "to do" list and your day is off to a great start!

*"Be willing to be a beginner every single morning."*

MEISTER ECKHART

Before you go to bed think about your challenges and then let your subconscious work on them while you sleep. You will be surprised how much more you can accomplish when you let your subconscious deal with your challenges, instead of letting fear rule you. Have you ever taken a test and you did not know the answer to a question, but the next day, all of a sudden, the answer just popped right into your head? Your subconscious was working on that problem the whole time. Your brain is an amazing tool. It is capable of so much more than we understand. When your mind sees a problem, mystery, or pattern it immediately goes on overdrive to fix, solve, or continue it. Success leaves trails and clues. Just like Hansel and Gretel did with their bread crumbs. You need to find and follow them.

*"The beginning is the most important part of the work."*

PLATO

I have my I Can Do It! coin. Every morning when I wake up, to get my day started, I pick up my I Can Do It! coin. I think of all the things I am grateful for, the things I am going to accomplish, the people I love, the people who teach me, and I become mindful of my journey. I carry my I Can Do It! coin with me. When I have fears or challenges, I grab my I Can Do It! coin and know that I am not alone and I am grateful for all I have. Then I continue on with my day with confidence. At night, before I go to bed, I once again take out my I Can Do It! coin and think of all the people and things I am grateful for. I think about what I have accomplished that day. My I Can Do It! coin helps to remind me to be the best, most amazing version of myself.

*"Knowing is not enough; we must apply. Willing is not enough; we must do."*

JOHANN W. VON GOETHE

So, let's get into the right mindset, hold your I Can Do It! coin, stand up and say: "I'm amazing! I can do it!"

Now, say it with confidence: " I'M AMAZING! I CAN DO IT!! "

Oh yeah, do a little dance and sing it this time: "I'M AMAZING! I CAN DO IT!!

*"If the only prayer you ever say in your entire life is thank you, it will be enough."*

MEISTER ECKHART

One more time: I'M AMAZING! I CAN DO IT!!

That was great! Give yourself a round of applause.

If you continue doing the same things, you will get the same results. It is only when you change what you are doing that your results will change. As you believe in yourself and begin to change, you will become a better version of yourself. In order to have a different life, you have to become an Amazing version of yourself. I want you to believe you are the butterfly. See yourself soaring to the top, reaching your goals and living the life you were meant to have.

# The Caterpillar

## CHRISTINA G. ROSSETTI

*Brown and furry*

*Caterpillar in a hurry;*

*Take your walk*

*To the shady leaf, or stalk.*

*May no toad spy you,*

*May the little birds pass by you;*

*Spin and die,*

*To live again a butterfly.*

Chapter 2

# ESCAPE
# YOUR FEAR

## TAKE THE CHAINS OFF
## AND BE EMPOWERED TO
## SUCCEED...

"All your dreams wait just on the other side of your fears."

– GRANT CARDONE–

Let's conquer your FEAR! In order to conquer your FEAR, you must first understand what FEAR is. Zig Ziglar would say "FEAR is False Expectations Appearing Real". It will take knowledge, love, and practice to overcome the fears that stand in your way.

Fear affects us all. We all experience Fear no matter if it is real or imagined. Most of us are afraid of the unknown. So the easiest way to conquer your Fear is to make the unknown known. This means to learn what we do not know. Luckily, for all of us, this is actually really easy. "How do you do it?" you ask? Well, you can read a book like you are doing right now. You can ask someone or take a class. You can watch a video on YouTube that explains a topic. You can even take the jump and try something new.

Did you know that often fear does us all more harm than the actual problem or situation? Do not give fear that power. Arm yourself and reach your potential by letting go of your fears and letting yourself overcome them.

# We Never Know How High We Are

(1176) EMILY DICKINSON

*We never know how high we are*
*Til we are called to rise;*
*And then, if we are true to plan,*
*Our statures touch the skies—*

*The Heroism we recite*
*Would be a daily thing,*
*Did not ourselves the Cubits warp*
*For fear to be King*

Sometimes other people try to make their fears your reality. For example, one day I was in line to go on my first loop-de-loop rollercoaster ride. I was so excited. I was finally tall enough to go on the ride. I stood in line with my Mom, waiting for my turn. The woman in front of me asked if I had ever been on the ride. I told her, "No." I was so excited, as this would be my first time. She then began to tell me all about how much she hated going upside down on the rollercoaster; how scary it is when you feel like you could fall out.

She said that the loop-de-loops made her sick. She was so surprised that I was excited to go on the ride, because she was so scared. The woman continued to go on and on about her fears of riding the rollercoaster, listing one after another. So, by the time I got to the front of the line, I no longer wanted to get on the ride. Her fears kept me from riding my first loop-de-loop rollercoaster ride that day. I chose to be convinced to be afraid. I let her fear overwhelm my intentions.

Some people fear the boogieman. Now, this may seem childish, but it comes from a real thing to fear. A long time ago, there were debtor's prisons. This meant when someone could not pay their bills, they would have to go to a work camp type of prison to work off their debt. Some people tell the story that in Germany, before the 20th century, if a family could not pay their rent or other debts, the debt collector would come to get the money owed. If the family did not have the money, the police would take the children to a work farm to work off the debt. So, parents would tell their children to quickly hide under the bed or in the closet because the burgermeister (boogie man) is coming.

Others tell the story that if you are bad, or do not go to bed on time, then the Boogie man will come from under your bed or out of the closet to take the bad kid away to a bad place. Today, these stories have no real value for us to fear them, but many people are still afraid of the boogieman.

When we learn the origin of these fears, often we can conquer them simply by understanding there is nothing to be afraid of.

I was afraid of heights. One day, my dad asked me if I would like to help him fix something on the playset. I said, "Yes," and we got the tools. My dad needed me to climb up on top of the playset and, from the top of the beam, screw the nut into the bolt he was holding below. We talked about the easiest, safest way for me to do it, but I was afraid of being up so high. My dad asked me what I was afraid of. I said, "I'm afraid of heights." He asked me if I had ever climbed on top of the playset and I said, "No." He then asked me how did I know I could not do it. Well, I did not have a good answer, so I agreed to try. We worked together as a team and I did it. I helped him.

At first, I was a little unsure. But then, as my dad encouraged me and I took one step and then another, I realized I wasn't afraid of heights. I just had not tried it before.

Many times, we are afraid of the unknown simply because it is unknown. There are days when you need a bit of faith in the universe to give you the strength and calmness to face difficult times. Keep in mind the wise words of the psalm written two thousand years ago. Repeat it in your mind and hold it dear to your heart. Sometimes you just have to have faith in a higher, stronger being.

*"Courage is knowing what not to fear"*

PLATO

*The Lord is my shepherd;*
*I shall not want.*
*He maketh me to lie down in green pastures:*
*he leadeth me beside the still waters.*

*He restoreth my soul:*
*he leadeth me in the paths of righteousness*
*for his name's sake.*
*Yea, though I walk through the valley*
*of the shadow of death,*
*I will fear no evil: for thou art with me;*
*thy rod and thy staff they comfort me.*

*Thou preparest a table before me*
*in the presence of mine enemies:*
*thou anointest my head with oil;*
*my cup runneth over.*
*Surely goodness and mercy shall follow me*
*all the days of my life: and I will dwell*
*in the house of the Lord for ever.—*

*Psalm 23:1-6*

Fear kills dreams; it can stop you, and paralyze you. Why? Because it stops you from taking the first step. Does this mean you should live recklessly and without any caution? NO. Putting your hand on a hot stove will burn your hand. Do not go down the dark alley in the middle of the night looking for problems or expecting that this will somehow prove you have no fear.

*"Limits, like fear, are often an illusion."*

**MICHAEL JORDAN**

> "Courage is resistance to fear, mastery of fear, not absence of fear."
>
> MARK TWAIN

There are things in life that you should be aware of that can harm you. Understand that things can hurt you. Not everyone is kind or helpful. Not everywhere is safe. If you are aware of people and situations that can cause real harm, then you can learn how to protect yourself or avoid them. It is important to know you can take action to overcome all your fears. This does not mean you will become FEARLESS; just successful. Embrace your fears. Once you learn to embrace your FEARs, you will have beaten them. It means you can grow and bloom into a better healthier, happier you.

Running from an imaginary fear will cause you to fall or get hurt, because it is imaginary and therefore you can never get away. What I am talking about is overcoming your fear so you can deal with what is real. You may have a fear of rejection, which most of us have. If you do not put yourself out there, you may still feel rejection, but you will never feel success.

> "You will miss the best things if you keep your eyes shut."
>
> DR. SEUSS

One day I was at an event with a whole bunch of kids having fun!!

There were two kids who were VERY SHY and NOT playing, or riding the ponies, or even petting the baby animals.

I tried ALL DAY to get them to have fun with me... and FINALLY, we all had a bunch of FUN. We rode the ponies, and I even got the kids to play with and hold the baby animals. One liked the bunny and the other liked the baby ducks best! I liked them both.

*"I have learned over the years that when one's mind is made up, this diminished fear; knowing what must be done does away with fear."*

**MARK TWAIN**

On the ride home, I asked my mom, "Why were those kids so shy?" She asked me what I meant.

I explained about the two kids and how SAD I was that we were not able to play more.

She then told me "Oh Sweetie, those kids were not shy. They just did not know how to ride a pony, or how to hold the animals; so they were afraid to try new things and their parents were afraid they might get hurt.

It made me MAD that FEAR had robbed us of being able to play and have FUN!

So I decided to make a YouTube series called "How Do You Do It?" Then, people could watch my videos and learn how to do something, and they would not be afraid and could have more FUN!!

*"If you want to conquer fear, don't sit at home and think about it. Go out and get busy"*

DALE CARNEGIE

What lies at the bottom of the ocean and shakes a lot?

A nervous wreck.

What is a ghosts' favorite dessert?

I-scream.

I have found laughter to be a great escape from fear because, when you are laughing, it is impossible to think about or do anything else.

*"Your future should scare you and excite you!"*

OMAR PERIU

Chapter 3

# ACCESS YOUR IMAGINATION

## LET IT FLOW, LET IT GROW, SEE YOUR GOALS...

*"If you can dream it,
you can do it."*

**– WALT DISNEY–**

Write down your goals. See yourself reaching them. Then you will start to make them real. Success begins in the mind. If you are not able to access your imagination in your mind, make a vision board. This is easy to do. Take pictures, draw pictures, cut pictures out of magazines. Then put them on your vision board. Allow yourself to go wild with imagination and fill the board with wonderful pictures. These pictures are clothes you want, people you want to meet, things you want to own, places you want to go, things you want to do, and so on. Once you get these creative juices flowing, then you will begin to be able to see them in your mind's eye too.

*"See it, believe it, achieve it. These are words I live by."*

ZIG ZIGLAR

It is so vital that you visualize your goals. This sounds simple enough, but what does it mean? Here are a few examples of me visualizing my goals, and then achieving them:

*"A goal not written down, is merely a wish."*

J LELAND DAVIS

One day I was reading a book called Skip. Skip, Skip. There was a little girl in it who did not know how to skip. Her mother helped her learn how to skip. After reading this book, I thought how fun it would be to skip. But I didn't know how to. I decided to close my eyes and visualize myself skipping up and down the hallway in my house. It made me smile as I pictured myself skipping about the house. I opened my eyes and I tried to skip up the hallway. That didn't go so well. So I closed my eyes and visualized myself skipping back down the hallway in my mind. Then I opened my eyes and tried again. It went much better this time. So one more time, I closed my eyes, and this time I saw myself skipping and smiling. It looked like fun. Next, I opened my eyes and started to skip. This time, I skipped all around the house. WoooHoo! I did it! I skipped!

*"All our dreams can come true if we have the courage to pursue them."*

**WALT DISNEY**

There is a song called

*"One Little Spark,"*

by RICHARD AND ROBERT SHERMAN
that talks about how,

*"One little spark, of inspiration*

*is at the heart, of all creation,"*

*and how,*

*"We all have sparks, imaginations;*

*that's how our minds,*

*create creations.*

*For they can make,*

*our wildest dreams come true;*

*those magic sparks, in me and you.*

*Imagination, imagination.*

*A dream, can be, a dream come true.*

*With just that spark, in me and you..."*

On a sunny day, I was outside with my dad. He was teaching me how to catch and throw a ball. He kept saying, "Keep your eye on the ball." I was trying, but it was not going too well. So he said, "Stop for a minute and come here. Let's close our eyes and see yourself catching the ball." I said, "Okay, I think I can." So, he threw the ball to me, I kept my eye on the ball, until it hit me in the chest. It did not really hurt, but I did not like it. So, I closed my eyes and saw my dad throwing the ball. I visualized the ball coming right into my hands and grabbing it. This made me smile. My dad threw me the ball again. I kept my eyes open and saw the ball coming right into my hands. Then I grabbed it. I caught the ball. I caught the ball! Now, it was time to throw it back. Well, I threw it all right. My dad said, "Next time, look at where you want the ball to go." I closed my eyes, saw myself throwing the ball to my dad, him catching it, and throwing it back to me. And I caught it every time. So, I tried again. I threw it right to him, and he quickly threw it back to me. We did it! I took a step backwards and we did it again. Wow, this is fun!

*"Setting goals is the first step to turning the invisible into the visible."*

**TONY ROBBINS**

Before my 4th birthday, my dad said, "I think it is time to take those training wheels off of your bike." "Oh no," I said, "I need them".

My dad told me, "You will be fine. It will just take some practice. See the other kids (bigger kids) riding their bikes". Oh, I saw the bigger kids riding their bikes, but I am smaller than them. He said, "I will be here to help you. We will do it tomorrow." Therefore, I took advantage of riding my bike as much as I could that day. Finally, it was dinnertime. At dinner, I talked with my dad about when he rode his bike without training wheels. He said he fell down, but he was okay. That night, before I went to sleep, I thought long and hard about tomorrow and riding my bike without training wheels. I closed my eyes and visualized riding my bike. I dreamed about it all night. When I woke up I told my dad all about my dream. So I said, "Okay let's do it." As my dad took the training wheels off, I closed my eyes and visualized me riding up and down the street on my bike. My dad said, "I will be right here helping you to balance. We started a little shaky and then it started to get easier. "Wow, dad, I think I can do it." I looked back to tell him to let go and he was not there, I was doing it. Oops I fell. My dad came over to help me, but I was okay. "I am ready to try again," I said. So, up on the bike I went again. I heard clapping. It was my mom. She said, "You are doing great!" I was; I was riding my bike without training wheels. I am a big boy now, I thought to myself.

I feel that everything happens twice. First, in the mind, as your thoughts, or what you visualize. Then, the second time, in reality, as what you do or create.

# Chapter 4

# MAKE YOUR PLAN

## WRITE IT DOWN...

*"If you fail to plan, you are planning to fail!"*

– **BENJAMIN FRANKLIN** –

The more detailed your plan, the easier it is to follow and the more like your picture it will look. Have you ever built blocks? I love to build blocks. Every time you stack them, they turn out just a little bit different. Sometimes I stack them as high as I can, and sometimes I stack them in squares. Sometimes I stack them just to knock them down. However, one day my mom asked my sister and me to build the blocks in a contest. Oh, I knew I could win. I thought I am going to build them high, just like the Empire State building. My sister thought she would build a model of Kennedy Space Center. We both built independent of each other. Then it was time for my mom to choose. Wow, we had both done such a great job. I had built the highest, and it looked like the Empire State building. My sister built a whole bunch of buildings and showed the whole Kennedy Space Center complex. Therefore, I won highest, and she won most creative. We each had a plan and they were very different, but we had the same blocks to build with.

I love to build Legos. It is important to know what you are building, make sure you have all the right parts, and follow the directions. Sometimes, I just want to be creative and take a few pieces and stick them together, and then some more. This is lots of fun, but it never looks like the picture when I build this way. I built a whole spaceport set one day. When I dumped out the entire box of Lego pieces and separated them into color groups, it did not look like a space port at all. As I followed the directions and checked the picture on the box, it started to look more and more like a spaceport. I later made lots of different things out of the same Legos, but when I had a clear plan and a good picture of what I wanted, then that is what I built every time.

For Christmas, one year, I got a big boy bike. My dad and godfather helped me to put it together. It was so much fun following the directions and finding the pieces. They joked around about how there were no pieces left over when we were finished. Even though, as we were building it, I was not sure where some of the pieces went, or why I would need them, it all made sense when we were finished. It looked just like the picture on the box. Oh, I was so excited to ride it. WOW, it was so much fun.

# Work

ANONYMOUS

*Work while you work,*

*Play while you play;*

*This is the way to be happy each day.*

*All that you do ,*

*Do with your might;*

*Things done by halves*

*Are never done right.*

How can you make seven even?

Remove the "S"

Do you know what the longest word in the dictionary is?

The word "smiles" because there is a      mile between each s.

*"It is better to be prepared for an opportunity and not have one, than to have an opportunity and not be prepared."*

**WHITNEY YOUNG, JR.**

# Chapter 5

# ACT ON YOUR PLAN

## AND NEVER GIVE UP...

"A river cuts through rock not because of its power, but because of its persistence."

— **JIM WATKINS** —

Sometimes, you do not know how you are going to do something, just that you want to do it. Other times you know how to do it, but it takes a lot of practice and maybe even some help to do it. You can do it; just keep on trying.

One day I was playing miniature golf with my family. There were little hints at each hole to help you to get the ball into the hole. At the first hole I put my ball down and it took five tries to get it in. My mom read the sign out loud: "The smugglers' tale can give you insight. Just aim for the wall behind the hole on the right." It only took her two tries. So, at the next hole I raced over and read the sign out loud: "Beware the water that lurks to the side. Stay tight to the left and in the hole you will ride." I made a plan to put the ball on the left side and tap it to the left. My ball rolled right by the slope and stopped next to the hole. Wow! I did well! Glad I had a plan. At the next hole it said, "A hint here would be "left and under"; hitting too hard would sure be a blunder." I made a plan to go through the middle and I hit the ball. When I got to the hole, I did not see my ball. My mom said, "Check the hole." I did, and I got a hole in one!!!!

*"Someone is sitting in the shade today because someone planted a tree a long time ago."*

**WARREN BUFFET**

*"Sometimes you have to believe in someone else's belief in you... until your own belief kicks in!"*

**LES BROWN**

*"Whether you think you can, or you think you can't—you're right."*

**HENRY FORD**

# A Lesson from History

## BY JOSEPH MORRIS

*Everything's easy after it's done;*
*Every battle's a "cinch" that's won;*
*Every problem is clear that's solved--*
*The earth was round when it revolved!*
*But Washington stood amid grave doubt*
*With enemy forces camped about;*
*He could not know how he would fare*
*Till after he'd crossed the Delaware.*
*Though the river was full of ice*
*He did not think about it twice,*
*But started across in the dead of night,*
*The enemy waiting to open the fight.*
*Likely feeling pretty blue,*
*Being human, same as you,*
*But he was brave amid despair,*
*And Washington crossed the Delaware!*
*So when you're with trouble beset,*
*And your spirits are soaking wet,*
*When all the sky with clouds is black,*
*Don't lie down upon your back*
*And look at them. Just do the thing;*
*Though you are choked, still try to sing.*
*If times are dark, believe them fair,*
*And you will cross the Delaware!*

*"Look at a stone cutter hammering away at his rock. Perhaps a hundred times without as much as a crack showing in it. Yet, at the hundred-and-first blow, it will split in two, and I know it was not the last blow that did it but all that had gone before."*

WHITNEY YOUNG, JR.

*"If I have seen further than others, it is by standing on the shoulders of giants."*

ISSAC NEWTON

When President Kennedy asked Dr. Wernher Von Braun what it would take to build a rocket that could carry a man to the moon and bring him back safely to the Earth, Von Braun answered him in five words, "The will to do it." Armed with this information on May 25, 1961, President John F. Kennedy announced his goal of putting a man on the moon by the end of the decade to a joint session of Congress and the world. In less than ten years, we accomplished this with the Apollo 11 flight, on July 20, 1969: The Moon Landing. Neil Armstrong and Buzz Aldrin landed, walked on the moon, and returned safely to Earth.

So let us look at this and break it down. What happened? President

> *"In order to succeed we must first believe we can."*
>
> **NIKOS KAZANTZAKIS**

> *"That's one small step for man, one giant leap for mankind"*
>
> **NEIL ARMSTRONG.**

Kennedy asked what it would take. He was answered with five simple words, "The will to do it." President Kennedy took his imagination and challenged us Americans to make his dream a reality, and do it within the next 10 years. Well, this showed us what we wanted to do, when we wanted to do it, and motivated us to make it happen. There were some failures and setbacks along the way, but we had the goal, the vision, the imagination, the plan to do it, and we never gave up! Not only did we reach our goal, but also we did it before we had set out to, and we did it five more times. The last was Apollo 17, which landed on the moon on December 7, 1972. Twelve men have walked on the moon and come home to tell us all about it.

> *"Our greatest weakness lies in giving up. The most common way to succeed is always to try just one more time."*
>
> **THOMAS A EDISON**

Did you hear about the cow astronaut?

Yeah he went to the mooooooooooooooon!

What goes up and never comes down?

Your age!

Did you hear about the great new restaurant on the moon?

The food is excellent, but there is no atmosphere.

*Mystery creates wonder and wonder is the basis of man's desire to understand."*

NEIL ARMSTRONG

What is an astronaut's favorite meal?

Launch!

*"Making your mark on the world is hard. If it were easy, everybody would do it. But it's not. It takes patience; it takes commitment; and it comes with plenty of failures along the way. The real test is not whether you avoid this failure, because you won't. It is rather you let it harden or shame you into inaction, or whether you learn from it; whether you choose to persevere."*

BARACK OBAMA

"Without goals, and plans to reach them, you are like a ship that has set sail with no destination."

FITZHUGH DODSON

"And will you succeed? Yes you will indeed! (98 and ¾ percent guaranteed.)"

Dr. Seuss

"Keep your eyes on the stars, and your feet on the ground."

THEODORE ROOSEVELT

Chapter 6

# ZEST FOR LIFE IS LEARNING

## LEARN SOMETHING NEW EVERY DAY...

"The more that you read, the more things you'll know. The more that you learn, the more places you'll go."

– DR. SEUSS –

Learn everything you can. Just get out there and do it - look, listen, learn. There is an importance of learning. You must understand what you learn so you can apply it. The more you learn, the better you can become.

*"Knowledge is the new Currency."*

LES BROWN

Life is a lot like a relay race.
Sometimes you start the race, or have an idea, and you need someone else to help you finish it. I love relays because one person starts it and then lots of other people work together to finish it. And then everyone is a winner!

*"Team Work Makes The Dream Work!"*

JOHN C. MAXWELL

Did you hear the one about the two silkworms who had a race?

It ended in a tie!

Did you hear about the race between the lettuce and the tomato?

The lettuce was a "head" and the tomato was trying to "ketchup"!

What kind of shoes are made from banana skins?

Slippers.

I love to learn new things and share them with others. I have always found it interesting how much you can learn by just being willing to learn and be taught. For example, one time I was at a seminar and I met a woman named Miss Angie. She was really nice. As we were talking, I told her I had online educational videos and loved to learn new things and share it with others. We talked some more and I found out she worked with the Great Mr. Les Brown. She told me about the wonderful opportunity Mr. Les Brown and the Les Brown Institute were providing to people who wanted to learn more and better themselves. I was interested. In addition, as you can see, I took advantage of this wonderful opportunity, and now I am speaking to audiences, working with the greats, and motivating people to be the best they can be.

*"Only I can change my life. No one can do it for me."*

CAROL BURNETT

I feel it is not only important to learn things, but also to share that knowledge with others. You never know what you can learn from someone. Knowledge is power and has always played a part in history. If used correctly, it can even change the course of history.

In 1776, there was a great man named George Washington. He was having a meeting with a Congressional committee. In the back of the room was a woman, and they were discussing how the American flag should be made. What should be on it? How should it be made? George Washington said, "I want stars. I want a six-pointed star like the Star of David." That woman in the back stood up and took a piece of paper, folded it, and with one scissor cut, she changed the course of our American flag. She had knowledge, and she explained that a five-point star could be easily uniformed and would work best. I think we recognize Betsy Ross's five-pointed star now, and know her name as well. She had knowledge; she used it, and shared it with others.

If you would like to make the 5 point star with one cut, here is an instruction sheet that shows you how to do it.

Thanks to the Betsy Ross House for providing these instructions.

## STEP 1

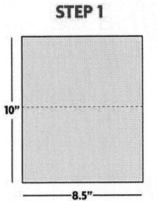

Fold an 8-1/2" x 10" piece of paper in half.

## STEP 2

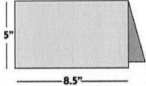

Fold and unfold that in half both ways to form creased center lines.

## STEP 3

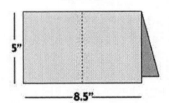

Bring corner (1) right to meet the center line. Be sure to fold from the vertical crease line.

## STEP 4

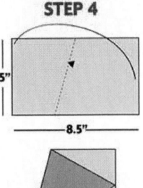

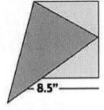

Bring corner (1) right till edges coincide, then make the fold.

## STEP 5

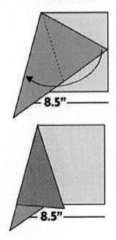

Bring corner (1) left and fold.

## STEP 6

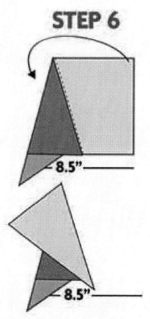

Flip project over. Bring corner (2) right until edges coincide. Then fold.

## STEP 7

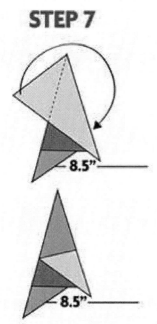

Bring right edge AC and the left edge AB together, crease, and unfold. Join points A and C, crease, and unfold.

## STEP 8

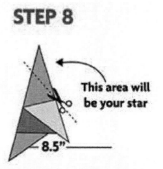

This area will be your star

Cut on the angle as shown in the picture (from point C, through the intersection of the fold lines from step 7, to the left edge). Then unfold the small piece.

## STEP 9

Marvel at your perfect five-pointed star! If your star is not perfect, take a fresh piece of paper (8-1/2" x 10" not 8-1/2" x 11") and return to Step 1.

# In 1492

## BY JEAN MARZOLLO

*In fourteen hundred ninety-two*
*Columbus sailed the ocean blue.*

*He had three ships and left from Spain;*
*He sailed through sunshine, wind and rain.*

*He sailed by night; he sailed by day;*
*He used the stars to find his way.*

*A compass also helped him know*
*How to find the way to go.*

*Ninety sailors were on board;*
*Some men worked while others snored.*

*Then the workers went to sleep;*
*And others watched the ocean deep.*

*Day after day they looked for land;*
*They dreamed of trees and rocks and sand.*

*October 12 their dream came true,*
*You never saw a happier crew!*

*"Indians! Indians!" Columbus cried;*
*His heart was filled with joyful pride.*

*But "India" the land was not;*
*It was the Bahamas, and it was hot.*

*The Arakawa natives were very nice;*
*They gave the sailors food and spice.*

Columbus sailed on to find some gold
To bring back home, as he'd been told.

He made the trip again and again,
Trading gold to bring to Spain.

The first American?  No, not quite.
But Columbus was brave, and he was bright.

"You will never discover new oceans
unless you have the courage to lose sight
of the shore."
ANDRÉ GIDE

"Your present circumstances don't
determine where you can go; they
merely determine where you start."
NIDO QUBEIN

"Nothing in the world can take the place of persistence. Talent will not; nothing is more common than unsuccessful men with talent. Genius will not; unrewarded genius is almost a proverb. Education will not; the world is full of educated derelicts. Persistence and determination alone are omnipotent. The slogan Press On! has solved and always will solve the problems of the human race."

CALVIN COOLIDGE

Chapter 7

# INNER CHILD

## NEEDS YOUR LOVE...

"*Whatever you would do as your younger self is what you should do today,*"

–GRANT CARDONE –

Remember when you could not wait for recess to go outside and play? How much fun you had swinging on the swings, sliding down the slide, and running around laughing and playing? Well your inner child still likes to run and play. Let it! Take a minute and dance like no one is watching. Truly let go and enjoy yourself. Have an ice cream. Watch a funny movie. Play outside. Laugh and joke. Get down on the floor and roll around. Give yourself a hug. Look in the mirror and see how great you really are. Remember to love yourself first.

We are born with this unique gift to love others and have fun. Somewhere along the way to adulthood, we seem to forget it.

Your inner child needs love too. Let yourself run and play, swing on the swings way up high. Slide down the slides, and yell out "Wheeeee!" It is important to nurture your inner child through positivity, imagination, and love.

Why do we put candles on top of a birthday cake?

Because it's too hard to put them on the bottom!

What did one candle say to the other?

"Don't birthdays burn you up?"

When is a birthday cake like a golf ball?

When it's been sliced.

What do you give a nine-hundred-pound gorilla for his birthday?

I don't know, but you'd better hope he likes it!

How does Moby Dick celebrate his birthday?

He has a whale of a party!

What was the average age of a cave man?

Stone Age!

# Perpetual Child

My Mom

*I am perpetual child*
*I am not naughty*
*I just want to stretch my legs*
*kick the sand*
*climb the tree*
*roam the land*
*swim the waters*
*and fly the sky*
*Who am I?*
*I am perpetual child*
*And I sleep in the lap of God.*

Do you remember the song

# "A Spoonful of Sugar"

by Richard M. Sherman & Robert B. Sherman? It was sung by Julie Andrews in the Disney Movie "Mary Poppins". In the song, she tells the children that,

*"In every job that must be done,*
*There is an element of fun*
*You find the fun and snap!*
*The job's a game*
*And every task you undertake*
*Becomes a piece of cake…"*

I think if you approach every task with this positive attitude, you will find that life can be a fun adventure.

Do you remember the clean-up game? Life is simply what you make it. The choice is yours.

You can choose to be happy and have fun, or you can choose not to.

It does not matter how much money you have, where you are, or even who you are with; only you can make yourself happy. Yes, all those things can help to make it easier or harder to make that choice; but the choice is yours.

I find it is easy to have fun. Every day, I find a mystery or adventure, and want to explore them. Why? I say it is because I like to have fun. My mom says it is easier for me, as a kid, because everything is a new adventure and new discovery. When I get the chance to meet a new friend, play a game, or go swimming (even if it is cold) I run, jump in, and make the most of it. I often encourage others to jump in too.

It is important to take the time to ask, "Why?" (maybe even a hundred times). You can see things differently, because of your perspective. The more you learn and understand how things work, your perspective or outlook on life changes. I think, as we get older, some people tend to forget why it is fun to roll on the ground or look up at the sky, but once they do it, they tend to remember.

I was lying down with my mom and sister on a dock looking at the clouds. Some looked like bunnies. Some were moving fast, just whisking by, and then I looked down and saw the reflections. Just then a dolphin passed by. My mom asked me why I was not looking up at the clouds and I said, "Sometimes when you are looking up, you will miss the wonders of down." In other words, do not keep your head in the clouds. There are wondrous things all around you.

Remember, your inner child can have fun doing just about anything. One time I wanted to play tag, but we were not supposed to run in the house, and it was raining outside. Well, we still played tag. We just played Zombie Tag (so no running). The adults even decided to play with us, once they stopped laughing. We had a great time.

*"The biggest adventure you can ever take is to live the life of your dreams."*

OPRAH WINFREY

When your inner child is having fun, there is something special that happens. It is almost like a glow that reaches out of you and surrounds you with positivity. I was playing at the park on a spinning ride. It is like a merry-go-round, but you push it by running around it while hanging on to it. Then jump on it and spin, spin, spin! I was having a lot of fun. There were four older kids. They were much older late teens, early twenties passing through the park. One walked right by me as I was starting to push the spinning ride. I said, "Excuse me, do you want to help push? It is fun!" He said, "Ok, sure." So we pushed it really fast and I said, "Ok let's jump on!" We did. WHEEEE! Once we stopped, I said, "Let's do it again!" I asked his friends if they wanted to do it too, and two more of them did it! Wow, we really went fast! One girl was just looking at the ground and not having fun, but we were all laughing and spinning. Once it stopped, I said, "Are you sure you don't want to try it?" Her friends all said, "Come on it's fun!" So she got on, and we did it again. She started smiling and laughing. They ended up staying and playing on the playground, smiling and having fun even after I had to leave.

When you look for the fun through the eyes of your inner child, everyday is an adventure. There is wonder and amazement to be found. Make it a game or a goal to find it! Here are some examples to get you started: What is the longest word? Solve a riddle or two? Think outside of the box, and then turn the box into a spaceship and blast off!

"It is fun to have fun, but you got to know how."

DR. SEUSS

# Chapter 8

# NEED TO HELP OTHERS

## BE HELPFUL!

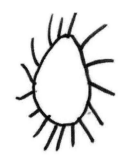

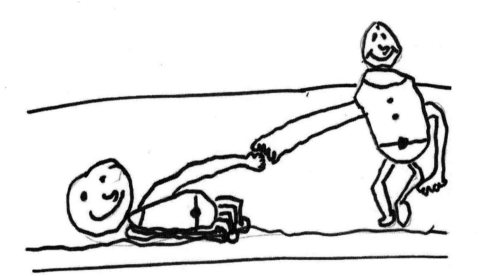

*"Alone we can do so little;*
*together we can do so much."*

– HELEN KELLER –

It is vitally important to help others; you do not have to be Wonder Woman or Superman. You just need to do the best you can. Be helpful – give a hand. Clean up and do your part. Be the ripple and turn into a wave.

Have you ever noticed when you smile at someone, they will usually smile back at you. When things are clean, they tend to stay clean. When you stop and help someone, it starts a chain reaction that grows much bigger than you could have done on your own? When you empower and inspire others, they do the same to others, too.

In order to help others, you must first help yourself. This means to take care of you first. This means, make sure you have a clean home, clean clothes, you eat well, and drink lots of water. You do not have to go out and cure cancer, or feed and clothe everyone. Just start by smiling, being helpful, doing what you can, and that can grow into curing cancer, or feeding and clothing everyone. Read a book to a child. Pick up a piece of trash on the ground. Give someone water. Donate old clothes and backpacks. Start with whatever you can.

Do you have a hobby or something you like to do? Is there an organization that could benefit from your expertise? Is there somewhere you could volunteer that would allow you to share your hobby with others? Is there a civic center or group you could join to be with likeminded individuals? Just getting out there and meeting new people is good.

*"Network equals your net worth."*

KEVIN HARRINGTON

I believe when we work together with others in collaborative, achievement driven relationships, great things can happen.

Be loving to the world, and nice to other people and animals. As you reach your goals give back. Be thankful for what you have. Enjoy the things you have and share them with others.

I enjoy going to hospitals and shelters where I read, do magic for kids, and give them goodies. One of the really cool things about giving, sharing, and helping is that you get this great feeling of accomplishment, and a happy feeling knowing you were able to make someone else's day better.

Once you have some security in your life, share your wealth, your love, and your knowledge with others. Pay it forward. This does not mean put yourself on the street by giving everything away. This means give what you can, be it money, time, whatever. It is amazing, the unique gifts we are all given. The more we share these gifts with others, the better everyone's lives can become.

Yes, in life there are takers and givers. I think it is better to give then to receive. But I do really like to get birthday gifts too!

A funny thing happens when you share, teach, and give of yourself. You receive joy, love, respect, admiration, etc. It is very rewarding to help others, especially those who are less fortunate.

What did the baby corn say to the mama corn?

"Where's Popcorn?"

Do you know what porcupines say when they kiss?

"Ouch"

What do you get when you cross a dog with an elephant?

A very nervous postman.

Do you know what you call a snowman in Florida?

A puddle

> *"When you point your finger at someone, anyone, it is often a moment of judgement. We point our fingers when we want to scold someone, point out what they have done wrong. But each time we point, we simultaneously point three fingers back at ourselves."*
>
> CHRISTOPHER PIKE

I have learned that no matter how good or how bad we have it, there is always someone who has it better, or someone who has it worse. So be thankful for what you have, and work to make it better.

Before you go to bed, take a minute to review the day. Reflect on all the things you can be thankful for. Be thankful for being alive, just for waking up one more day not six feet under. You can be thankful for the opportunity to feel the sunshine like a warm hug from God. Then share that thankfulness with others.

## Hearts Are Like Doors

### ANONYMOUS

*Hearts, like doors, will open with ease,*

*To very, very little keys,*

*And don't forget that two of these*

*Are "Thank you, sir" and "If you please!"*

"*Love is the condition in which the happiness of another person is essential to your own.*"

ROBERT A HEINLEIN

Chapter 9

# GOOD TIMES

WILL COME WHEN YOU
CHOOSE TO HAVE FUN...

"Folks are usually about as happy as they make their minds up to be."

– ABRAHAM LINCOLN –

Good times will come when you choose to have fun… live, love, and laugh. Laugh and have fun. Show your Smile to the world.

Celebrate all the little "high fives" of life. The more your recognize these small accomplishments, the more you will have, and the bigger they will get!

It is funny in life how people experiencing the same thing can have very different views of the event. Some people will find it to be ho hum; others scary; some interesting; others still, life changing. I asked my mom, "How is that possible?" She tried to explain it to me, but I really did not understand until one time I was at an event. I had so much fun laughing, screaming, and celebrating. It was a "best day ever" event for me.

While I was having fun, I looked around and some people were on their phones texting; others sleeping; and some were even crying. I thought to myself, "Are these people really here? How is it I am having such a great time and these other people are not?" That is when my mom told me that having fun is a choice.

*"For every minute you are angry, you lose 60 seconds of happiness"*

RALF WALDO EMMERSON

You can choose to have fun or you can choose to be miserable. If you choose to be miserable, recognize you are being miserable. Then you can make a better choice. Before you judge someone else, look at yourself. Make sure you are doing everything you want to and should be doing. Then understand you can never truly know what someone else is going through. My mom says, "Even if you could walk a mile in someone else's shoes, you still would not be where their feet have been."

We only get so many moments. Each of us has a secret set amount. Some of us only get a few, while others seem to get millions. I think it is not the number, or amount, we should worry about. It is the good time memories. If you enjoy and celebrate all of them, then you will have a great life! Relax and enjoy the moments you have.

*"Life is short and unpredictable. Eat the dessert first."*
HELEN KELLER

Do you know what was the most popular dance in 1776?

Indepen-dance

Did you hear the one about the Liberty Bell?

Yeah, it cracked me up too!

What does the Statue of Liberty Stand for?

'cause it can't sit down!

If you are laughing, it is hard to be scared, sad, or even think. You become truly present in the moment. Enjoy the moment! Show your smile to the world.

Whether you are a glass half full or a glass half empty person, it does not matter. You can still choose to celebrate. Either way, you're half way there!

*"Don't cry because it is over. Smile because it happened."*
DR. SEUSS

> *"Time you enjoy wasting is not wasted time."*
>
> MARTHE TROLY-CURTIN

When I go to the store and there are flowers, I stop and smell them. My mom and I stop and smell them. We pick out which ones are the best. Sometimes, the ones that look the best do not smell as nice as another bunch. Sometimes we buy some, and other times we just smell them and go about our shopping. Either way, we enjoy stopping and smelling the flowers.

As my Nana got older, we decided to celebrate half birthdays. I really enjoyed this 'cause it meant more cake for me. But for her, it meant she got to celebrate more birthdays with me. Now that she is gone, I am very happy we celebrated so many birthdays together.

> *"Don't cry because it is over. Smile because it happened."*
>
> DR. SEUSS

# BE AMAZING!

Don't be afraid to try new things. You can reach for the stars or even go to Mars.
Here is the secret to why you can **BE AMAZING**.

Your mind is already set up to be a digital camera, a digital video recorder, and a computer.

You can imagine and practice doing anything, seeing yourself accomplishing something you have never done before.

This is why you can do anything you set your mind to!

The more you practice this, the easier it gets.

You can do it, **BE AMAZING!**

# BE AMAZING
## Song

JOHN R.F. HUMPHREYS

*B.E... A.M.A.Z.I.N.G.*
*Be Amazing with John John.*
*Be Amazing with John John.*
*Just say I can, I can.*

*B   Begin by believing and build on it, '*
*cause once you see it, you can achieve it.*

*E   Escape your fear; take the chains off,*
*be empowered to succeed.*
*It will take knowledge, love and practice.*
*Let's conquer your fears with knowledge,*
*love and practice.*

*B.E... A.M.A.Z.I.N.G.*
*Be Amazing with John John.*
*Be Amazing with John John.*
*Just say I can, I can.*

*A   Access your imagination; let it flow;*
*let it grow; see your goals.*
*See yourself reaching them –*
*then you'll start to make them real.*

*M   Make a plan; write it down.*
*A goal not written down is just a wish.*
*Is Just A Wish.*

*A   Act on your plan and never give up.*
*Hold on tight and keep on climbing.*

*Unleash the 3 P's - passion, perseverance, and practice.*
*Passion, perseverance, and practice*

*B.E... A.M.A.Z.I.N.G.*
*Be Amazing with John John.*
*Be Amazing with John John.*
*Just say I can, I can.*

*Z   Zest for life is learning.*
*Learn something new every day.*
*Learn everything you can.*
*Just get out there and do it - look, listen, learn;*
*look, listen, learn.*

*I   Inner child needs your love.*
*Let yourself run and play.*
*Swing on the swings; fly up high.*
*Slide down the slide; yell out Wheeeee!*

*N   Need to help others;*
*you don't have to be Wonder Woman or Superman;*
*you just need to do the best you can.*
*Be helpful – give a hand; clean up.*
*Clean up and do your part.*
*Be the ripple and turn into a wave.*
*Turn into a wave.*

*G   Good times will come when you choose to have fun...*
*live, love, and laugh.*
*Laugh and have fun;*
*Show your smile to the world.*

*B.E... A.M.A.Z.I.N.G.*
*Be Amazing with John John.*
*Be Amazing with John John.*
*Just say I can, I can.*

# BE AMAZING
## Workbook

**A guide to becoming the best version of yourself.**
## WORKBOOK

**B**    Begin by believing and build on it...

**E**    Escape your FEAR, take the chains off...

**A**    Access your imagination, let it flow, let it grow, see your goals...

**M**    Make a plan, write it down...

**A**    Act on your plan and never give up...

**Z**    Zest for life is learning; learn something new every day...

**I**    Inner child needs your love...

**N**    Need to help others, be helpful...

**G**    Good Times will come when you choose to have fun...

# BE AMAZING
A guide to becoming the best version of yourself.

## WORKBOOK

**B**     Begin by believing and build on it…

| Decide to do something Like be the best version of yourself or make a million dollars… |
|---|
| |

| Evaluate where you are:. |
|---|
| |

| | | | |
|---|---|---|---|
| Are you happy? | | YES | NO |
| Are you smiling? | | YES | NO |
| Are you having fun? | | YES | NO |
| Are you working towards your goals? | | YES | NO |
| Are you contributing? | | YES | NO |

| If Yes, continue | | If No, regroup and make a change. | |
|---|---|---|---|
| | | | |

| Revaluate where you are:. |
|---|
| |

Treat each day like Christmas!
It is called the present, because it is a gift!

Start your day with a sense of
accomplishment, gratitude, and happiness.

| Use the BE AMAZING Things To Do (TTD) Daily Checklists |
|---|
| Use the BE AMAZING GOALS Worksheets |

*"Be willing to be a beginner
every single morning."*

- MEISTER ECKART -

# BE AMAZING
A guide to becoming the best version of yourself.

## WORKBOOK

**E**    Escape your FEAR, take the chains off…

| What are you afraid of? |
| --- |
|  |

| | | | |
| --- | --- | --- | --- |
| Is this a real thing? | | Or imagined? | |
| Is this a healthy fear? | | Or unhealthy fear? | |
| Is this your fear? | | Or someone else's fear? | |

Fear kills dreams.
There are things in life that you should be aware of and use caution.

| What can you do to become more informed about and overcome your fear? |
| --- |
|  |

| | | | |
| --- | --- | --- | --- |
| Read a book? | | Ask someone? | |
| Take a class? | | Get help? | |
| Face it? | | Practice? | |

Most fears actually do more harm than the actual problem.

It is important to understand that things can hurt you and not everyone is kind or helpful. Once you are aware of this, you can learn how to protect yourself and overcome those fears too.

*"Courage is knowing what not to fear."*

- PLATO -

# BE AMAZING

A guide to becoming the best version of yourself.

## WORKBOOK

**A**      Access your imagination let it flow, let it grow, see your goals...

Visualize your goals!

It is so important to visualize your goals; to see yourself achieving them.

| What are your goals? |
|---|
| Write them down in present tense twice a day. |
| |
| |
| |

| Use the BE AMAZING GOALS Sheet |
|---|

| Review your goals each day. |
|---|
| Once in the morning when you get up, and once before you go to bed. |

| Close your eyes and really see yourself reaching and enjoying your goals. |
|---|

| | |
|---|---|
| What does it feel like? | |
| What does it smell like? | |
| What does it sound like? | |
| Who is there with you? | |

## *"See it, believe it, achieve it."*

- ZIG ZIGLAR -

# BE AMAZING

A guide to becoming the best version of yourself.

## WORKBOOK

**M**    Make a plan, write it down…

The more detailed your plan the easier it is to follow.

| What are your goals? |
|---|
|  |
|  |

| When do you want to do/achieve it by? | | |
|---|---|---|
| Date | | Time |

| Is this a realistic goal? | | YES | | NO |
|---|---|---|---|---|
| Is this a realistic timeframe? | | YES | | NO |
| Do you need help to do it? | | YES | | NO |

| What resources do you need to do it? | YES | | NO |
|---|---|---|---|
|  | | | |

| Can you break the steps down further? | YES | | NO |
|---|---|---|---|
|  | | | |
|  | | | |

| Can you break the steps down further? | YES | | NO |
|---|---|---|---|
|  | | | |
|  | | | |

| Put the steps on a calendar so you can see the timeframe. |
|---|
|  |

*"If you fail to plan, you are planning to fail!"*

- BENJAMIN FRANKLIN -

# BE AMAZING
A guide to becoming the best version of yourself.

## WORKBOOK

**A**    Act on your plan and never give up…

Start working the steps and feeling the satisfaction of accomplishment.

If a step takes longer than expected, do not be discouraged.

Celebrate your accomplishments, and then move on to the next step.

| | | | | | |
|---|---|---|---|---|---|
| Review your plan and change it if necessary. | | | | | |
| Do you still want to do/achieve this? | | YES | | NO | |
| Do you need to adjust your timeframe? | | YES | | NO | |
| Date | | Time | | | |
| Is this a realistic goal? | | YES | | NO | |
| Do you need more help to do it? | | YES | | NO | |
| | | | | | |
| Do you need more resources to do it? | | YES | | NO | |
| | | | | | |
| What steps do you need to take? | | YES | | NO | |
| | | | | | |
| Can you break the steps down further? | | YES | | NO | |
| | | | | | |
| Put the steps on a calendar so you can work them. | | | | | |
| | | | | | |

## *"Whether you think you can, or you think you can't – you're right"*

- HENRY FORD-

# BE AMAZING
A guide to becoming the best version of yourself.

## WORKBOOK

**Z**    Zest for life is learning. Learn something new every day...

Read for at least 20 minutes a day. Pick books that are helpful and positive to read. It is fun to read fact and fictional books. The more variety you read, the more perspectives you get.

You can turn your car into a traveling classroom, by listening to audio books.

When you meet someone new, ask them questions. Here are some suggestions:

| What is the best piece of advice you have ever received? | |
| --- | --- |
| | |

| What do you do? | |
| --- | --- |
| Do you like what you do? | |
| What type of education and training requirements does your job have? | |

| What hobbies do you have? |
| --- |
| |
| What got you interested in it? |
| |

| Do you travel? | |
| --- | --- |
| Where do you like to go? | |
| Why do you enjoying traveling there? | |

## *"Knowledge is the new currency."*
- LES BROWN -

# BE AMAZING

A guide to becoming the best version of yourself.

# WORKBOOK

**1**  Inner child needs your love…

It is important to nurture your inner child through positivity, imagination, and love.

Let yourself run and play; smell the flowers and roll in the grass.

Look in the mirror and see how great you are; give yourself a hug.

| | |
|---|---|
| What makes you smile? | |
| What makes you laugh? | |
| What is your favorite joke? | |
| Schedule time each day just to play. | |

| | |
|---|---|
| Get outside and get in touch with nature. | |
| Sit outside, close your eyes, and imagine. | |
| Now see the world through your loving innocent eyes. | |

Happiness comes from within.
Money can't buy it, and no one can give it to you or take it away.

| | | | |
|---|---|---|---|
| Swing on the swings. | | Spin on the merry-go-round. | |
| Play the hot lava game. | | Don't step on a crack. | |
| Hop or skip instead of walking. | | Jump in even if the water is cold. | |
| Go on an adventure every day. | | Have fun no matter what you are doing. | |

*"The biggest adventure you can ever take is to live the life of your dreams."*

- OPRAH WINFREY -

# BE AMAZING
A guide to becoming the best version of yourself.

# WORKBOOK

**N** Need to help others, Be helpful...

| How can you help others? |
| --- |
| |
| What do you have or know that can help someone else? |
| |
| Who do you know that needs help? |
| |
| How can you help them? |
| |
| What are you thankful for? |
| |
| |
| |

First you must take care of yourself; you cannot give from an empty cup. When you help and inspire others, they will inspire others too.

| What do you like to do? |
| --- |
| |
| Is there somewhere you could volunteer and do that? |
| |
| We all have unique gifts and talents. What is yours? |
| |
| How can you share your gifts and talents with the world? |
| |

| Pick up some trash on the ground and throw it away. |
| --- |
| Smiling is contagious; share your smile! |

*Alone we can do so little; together we can do so much."*

- HELEN KELLER -

# BE AMAZING

A guide to becoming the best version of yourself.

## WORKBOOK

**G** Good Times will come when you choose to have fun…

What have you done today that made you smile?

|  |
|---|
|  |
|  |
|  |

Celebrate it! Reward yourself. Enjoy the high fives of life.
Do something you can be proud of.

| | |
|---|---|
| Forgive someone, especially if that someone is yourself | |
| Let go of something that is bothering you. | |

| | | | |
|---|---|---|---|
| Are you a glass half-full | | or half-empty person? | |

Either way you have a unique way of looking at things.
That should be celebrated!

| | |
|---|---|
| It is important to understand that people view things differently. | |
| Try to see things from different perspectives and points of view. | |

| | | | |
|---|---|---|---|
| Get down on the floor. | | Climb a ladder | |
| Ride an elevator way up high | | Ride a rollercoaster. | |
| Go on a merry-go-round. | | Slide down a slide. | |

Do what it takes to change your perspective and have fun.

*"It is fun to have fun, but you got to know how."*

- DR. SEUSS -

# BE AMAZING
# TTD Worksheets

**A guide to becoming the best version of yourself.**

**B**    Begin by believing and build on it...

**E**    Escape your FEAR, take the chains off...

**A**    Access your imagination, let it flow, let it grow, see your goals...

**M**    Make a plan, write it down...

**A**    Act on your plan and never give up...

**Z**    Zest for life is learning; learn something new every day...

**I**    Inner child needs your love...

**N**    Need to help others, be helpful...

**G**    Good Times will come when you choose to have fun...

# Things To Do (TTD) List Worksheet

Write and check off your TTD
In the morning.

| Things To Do | Sun | Mon | Tues | Wed | Thu | Fri | Sat |
|---|---|---|---|---|---|---|---|
| | | | | | | | |
| Wake Up | | | | | | | |
| Get up & make bed | | | | | | | |
| Brush your hair & teeth | | | | | | | |
| Get Dressed | | | | | | | |
| I Can Do It! coin | | | | | | | |
| Eat breakfast | | | | | | | |
| Review your Goals & TTD List | | | | | | | |
| Write out your Goals (Present Tense) | | | | | | | |

# Things To Do (TTD) List Worksheet

Write and check off your TTD
In the morning.

| Things To Do | Sun | Mon | Tues | Wed | Thu | Fri | Sat |
|---|---|---|---|---|---|---|---|
| | | | | | | | |
| Get ready for your day | | | | | | | |
| Be Helpful | | | | | | | |
| Learn something new | | | | | | | |
| Laugh & have fun | | | | | | | |
| | | | | | | | |
| | | | | | | | |
| | | | | | | | |
| | | | | | | | |
| | | | | | | | |
| | | | | | | | |
| | | | | | | | |

# Things To Do (TTD) List Worksheet

Write and check off your TTD
In the evening.

| Things To Do | Sun | Mon | Tues | Wed | Thu | Fri | Sat |
|---|---|---|---|---|---|---|---|
| | | | | | | | |
| Review your Goals & TTD List | | | | | | | |
| Write your Goals (Present Tense) | | | | | | | |
| Write your Daily TTD List | | | | | | | |
| Think about all the high fives | | | | | | | |
| Take a shower or bath | | | | | | | |
| Brush your teeth & hair | | | | | | | |
| Get ready for bed | | | | | | | |
| | | | | | | | |
| | | | | | | | |
| | | | | | | | |
| | | | | | | | |

# Things To Do (TTD) List Worksheet

Write and check off your TTD
In the evening.

| Things to Do | Sun | Mon | Tues | Wed | Thu | Fri | Sat |
|---|---|---|---|---|---|---|---|
| | | | | | | | |
| I Can Do It! coin | | | | | | | |
| Think about your challenges with a solution mind | | | | | | | |
| Let Go – Relax & Release | | | | | | | |
| Get a good night's rest | | | | | | | |
| Laugh & have fun | | | | | | | |
| | | | | | | | |
| | | | | | | | |
| | | | | | | | |
| | | | | | | | |

# BE AMAZING
## Goals Worksheets

**A guide to becoming the best version of yourself.**

**B**  Begin by believing and build on it…

**E**  Escape your FEAR, take the chains off…

**A**  Access your imagination, let it flow, let it grow, see your goals…

**M**  Make a plan, write it down…

**A**  Act on your plan and never give up…

**Z**  Zest for life is learning; learn something new every day…

**I**  Inner child needs your love…

**N**  Need to help others, be helpful…

**G**  Good Times will come when you choose to have fun…

# Goals Worksheet

Write your GOALS in present tense.
In the morning.

| For Example: I make good grades. |
| --- |
|  |
|  |
|  |
|  |
|  |
|  |
|  |
|  |
|  |
|  |
|  |
|  |
|  |
|  |
|  |
|  |
|  |
|  |
|  |
|  |
|  |
|  |
|  |
|  |
|  |

# Goals Worksheet

Write your GOALS in present tense.
In the evening.

| For Example: I am helpful. |
| --- |
| |
| |
| |
| |
| |
| |
| |
| |
| |
| |
| |
| |
| |
| |
| |
| |
| |
| |
| |
| |
| |
| |
| |
| |
| |
| |
| |

# INDEX

**A**

Activities

Betsy Ross's Five-pointed star  65

**B**

I Can Do It! coin 31

**P**

Poems

A Lesson from History  56

Hearts Are Like Doors  83

IN 1492  67

Perpetual Child  74

The Caterpillar  32

We never know how high we are (1176) 35

Work  52

**S**

Songs

A Spoonful of Sugar by Richard M. Sherman & Robert B. Sherman 74

BE AMAZING Song by John R. F. Humphreys 91

One Little Spark by Richard and Robert Sherman 46

**V**

Verses

The Lord is my shepherd 37

**W**

Worksheets

BE AMAZING - Workbook  93
BE AMAZING – Goals 109
BE AMAZING – TTD 103

# NOTES

# BE AMAZING

# GLOSSARY

It is important to never go past a word you do not understand.

Please use a dictionary if you find a word you do not understand.

It is important to always have a dictionary with you when you read.

It can even be just a phone with internet access, so you can look up any word you need to.